CW01514666

Start In The Middle

(Then read both ways!)

by

Colin Field

**Grosvenor House
Publishing Limited**

All rights reserved
Copyright © Colin Field, 2011

Colin Field is hereby identified as author of this
work in accordance with Section 77 of the Copyright, Designs
and Patents Act 1988

The book cover picture is copyright to Inmagine Corp LLC

This book is published by
Grosvenor House Publishing Ltd
28-30 High Street, Guildford, Surrey, GU1 3HY.
www.grosvenorhousepublishing.co.uk

This book is sold subject to the conditions that it shall not, by way of
trade or otherwise, be lent, resold, hired out or otherwise circulated
without the author's or publisher's prior consent in any form of binding or
cover other than that in which it is published and
without a similar condition including this condition being imposed
on the subsequent purchaser.

A CIP record for this book
is available from the British Library

ISBN 978-1-908105-48-6

Acknowledgements

My sincere thanks go to the following people. Without each and everyone of them, this book would never have been written.

Top of the list must be my good friend Ian Pickering, 'Old Pick' who insisted that I help him write a children's pantomime for Christmas in Lagos. He sparked an interest in writing that never left me.

Brenda Ogilvie who gave me so much help with her frank comments and critiques. She claims to know nothing about poetry. Maybe, but she goes on 'getting it right' time after time.

Dr. Christine Gadd who has been my GP for over 20 years. She kept me going many times when it would have been so much easier to give up.

John Lodge, whose conversations, particularly about art and poetry, kept my feet on the ground when my head was in the clouds.

My family, all of them. They are all very special and all have helped me, often without realising. In particular I must mention Claire-Lise, who critiqued the Christmas poems and Nicky who critiqued everything I showed her and was always there for me.

Finally, the most important person in my life, my inspiration, Jan, my lover and companion.

Contents

MEMORIES

It seems to me that the following poem applies to everyone.
If it does not then it is a shame!

MEMORIES

The memories crowd in upon me.
They hook into my heart.
There is no way to keep them out.
Nor would I try, nor stand apart.
Shining, crystal, clear, welcome drops
falling on my conscious mind.
Each one pure and oh, so precious.
These are the jewels of life, of love
Each one, more valued, than the one before.
Every one so beautiful, so full of joy.
Catch the throat,
bite back the tears,
grateful tenderness.

I don't know how to properly introduce this poem.
My father died when I was working overseas. I was
working in Pakistan on an emergency job and my
company denied me leave of absence. In those days
you were not automatically permitted to take time
off for funerals and in any case, not only I did not have
sufficient funds to purchase the tickets, his wife, my
stepmother, insisted on a swift funeral. I could not have
returned on time. So I buried my grief and tried to forget.
It was years later when I read a eulogy for my wife's Father
that all the bottled grief came flooding out. The poem that
follows was written soon after. Every time I read it, I weep.
The memories are as raw now, as they were 30 years ago.

MEMORIES OF MY FATHER

I remember my Dad with tears in my eyes.
He used to show me how to mend my old bike.
How to fix the roof on an underground camp;
so the fire didn't smoke.

My Dad smoked a pipe all the time,
even in the morning before he got out of bed.
His bedroom had a special smell and I loved it
and I wish he were with me now.
He walked out
when he caught my Mum with another man,
and he never even put up a fight;
just left my brother and me.
I left as soon as I could,
but my brother was too young.

My Dad went to live with my Gran.
Sometimes I went there to stay.
My Gran used to call my Dad, George.
We had bread with cheese and raw onion with cocoa for Supper,

about ten o'clock.
Then down to the outside privy, cold and smelly,
before going to bed.
He was very lonely without my mum.
He used to have a regular woman
at the back of St. Peter's churchyard.
After dark; in among the gravestones.

Years later, he got married again,
to a lonely lesbian, who wanted respectability:
but definitely no sex!
Well not the proper kind anyway.

My Dad used to meet me in pubs, after he married again.
I went to university then into my first job.
When I became a manager, our meetings were awkward.
There came a time when I was promoted.
He told me I was earning more than him.
And he wasn't happy for me.

Angry pride meant I didn't see him after that,
for many years.
Until my youngest daughter fixed a meeting;
without telling me.
We met, and he held my hand.
He was so tiny. Illness had wasted him away.
With every second word, he fought for breath.
His lungs had gone.

He loved my children and was proud for me.
We were friends again, extra special.
I never told him I loved him;
there was no need; he knew.
Two months later he died.
I was away in a foreign land and could not grieve at
his funeral.
But I remember my Dad. Every day.

*Doug was a wonderful man who would do anything
for anyone. He had a heart transplant and bad lungs.
Nevertheless he was managing well until his wife died. Then
he fell apart and it seemed as if he no longer cared to live.
That is until he met a lonely divorcee and he fell in love again.
He was granted a few weeks of happiness and then his illness
struck him down. He was laying in hospital when this next
poem was written for him.*

FOR DOUG!

Her husband was mad to drive her away.
Crazy to let her go.
Now she's yours, she is for you
No matter what, your luck has turned
And you are blessed.

Life has not been kind to you
Has dealt some rotten hands.
But she loves you, she loves you.
Do you realise what that means?

It means you have to fight and fight,
To beat the illness within.
You must be well, be strong again
Just do it all for her.

The two of you have a life to live
new happiness to grasp.
An example to give to those who care.
For both of you: be what you are.

Don't let this illness beat you
Fight for the life you deserve
Fight for the love of your woman.
Fight for the friends that you have.

*I was fourteen when my Mother betrayed my
Father. My relationship with her was difficult from then
on. No matter how I tried, I could not forgive her
and yet neither could I completely sever the bond.
My conflicting feelings tore me apart. She became
very religious as she sought forgiveness and reconciliation.
I hope that she found peace of mind.*

MEMORIES OF MY MOTHER

You gave me a Bible,
I gave you a poem.
An exchange of gifts,
but not in the home.

Too long apart,
now almost too late.
Was it stubborn insensitivity,
or just cruel fate?

We stayed apart,
thinking such bitterness.
The wasted years,
empty at best.

Now God's mercy,
has given us time together.
Before his greater priority,
and we can soothe the wounds

All my life I have hidden my fear and lack of confidence behind a bold façade. Despite this, I have had a wild, interesting life in many parts of the globe. The following is not great poetry but it does sum up my feelings in plain, simple language.

PAST EXPLOITS

I want to go to bed and dream of nothing;
just sleep a thousand nights.
Who needs to remember exploits past,
or fight a thousand fights.
I've travelled far and travelled long.
I've never been afraid.
I've seen the best; I've seen the worst,
and seen the price is paid.
But now the spirit weakens
The shades begin to call,
And I grow weary of the fight,
And worry for my soul.

My best friend died suddenly. I saw the anguish of his wife and how the only thing that really helped her were deep imaginary conversations with her late husband.

I MISS YOU

I can't touch you any more.
I can't hear you any more.
I can't see you any more.
But I can talk to you!
And sometimes I sense that you answer me
As time passes the sharp sense of loss.
Never fades
Unlike your face.
Which increasingly loses focus.

So I cling to that moment of time,
Captured in your photograph.
Which itself is already fading.
But I can still talk to you.

Here we go again, still fighting my fears! It would be easy to dismiss this poem as a piece of maudlin nonsense, but it does accurately reflect how I felt in my late fifties.

WHEN WE ARE ALMOST OLD

And now that we are almost old
yet love each other still.
Will all our pleasures stay with us
Or life take its vengeful fill?
Must we pay for happiness past?
Accept that things must end?
No my love, we will live on,
and love each other more.
We will continue with the fight
and laugh at victories won.
We will share our sorrows in defeat
and mourn about the loss.
But we will be together,
forever and forever
Until we die.

I have become more content and
'at peace' in my mid seventies.

PEACE IN RETIREMENT

Now we have passed seventy-four,
We should not worry anymore.
All life's problems are behind us.
We can enjoy loving, comfortable friendship,
Being together, better than apart.
We can recall a life full of rich experience.
Refuse to see the aging faults of body or mind.
Allow diminishing ambition to give greater contentment.
We do not need to care what people think,
but only to care how friends and family feel.
We have no further battles, no wars to win.
So the worst that life can throw at us now,
Is Death?
Is that really so bad?
For when the good lord takes us,
We will go together and be at peace.

*I wrote this when I was very low and not too sure
if I even wanted to live. What follows is pure
imagination! It does not reflect the events in my
life in any way. However writing the poem
did help me a great deal.*

"DEATH MY FRIEND, MY ENEMY."

So here it is. Death at last.
Hello friend, make it fast.
There's nothing to stay for
No one to care
Wanting to go
Afraid to remain
Enjoy the peace
Freedom from pain.

Long ago you took my wife
Who was my strength, my love, my life.
Together, we were a perfect match
Pleasure from the slightest touch.
I had three daughters, full of life
Perfect copies of my lovely wife.
Fate took them away, no thought or care
No looking back, emotion stripped bare.
But I still love them, care too much
Need to remember, want to touch.
Their support was mutual, their trust sublime
They loved their Father, their God benign.

They would want for me to stay
Fight my grief, not quit away.
So my friend, let go your grasp
Leave me now, your chance has passed.
I am not ready to die,
I've things I must do
Battles to win, places to go.

So keep your peace, your freedom from pain.
Those things aren't for me, I'm starting again.
To live a bit more and love a bit more
New wife, new life, maybe rapture in store
But I'll never forget, the one that you took
I'll carry forever her last dying look,
And remember the love, the joy that she gave,
And I will miss her 'til I enter my grave.

The following poem was inspired by the tragedy that occurred to a friend of mine. He made a mistake, he was wrong, but he did not deserve what happened to him.

HAVE PITY

Time presses down upon me
The shades can hardly wait.
I am too old to suffer
upon a woman's whim.
Why must you do me sorrow
for just one small mistake?
Have pity on my weakness,
or else my heart will break.

I cannot lie, though I may try
My capture is complete.
It is within your power to make
my waning years so sweet.
A smile and a few kind words
will make my sorrows cease.
You may take my years of wisdom,
my experience of life.
Just look upon me kindly,
My sweet and lovely wife.

It was a great loss when my mother-in Law died.
She was much loved and respected by all the family. She was
born in Wales and was proud of her Welsh heritage. My
father-in-law was Irish with all the virtues of a good
Irishman. He died well before mother-in-law and although it
was clear that she missed him she nevertheless bore her grief
and loneliness with cheerful courage and fortitude.
The following two poems are my tribute to them
and to help assuage the deep grief of the whole
family and my wife in particular.

SHE WILL NOT BE FORGOTTEN

She will not be forgotten,
Good people never are.
And so when you remember.
Recalling the things she did
And all that meant for you.
Then those memories will soothe
Your empty aching heart
She would not want you looking back
Grieving for what might have been
But rather would say: look forward
Build your family, always the family
Stay true to her ideal. Remember how she started
How she advanced her family using Welsh values
Attached to her Husbands Irish wit
and kind intentions.

Rejoice that they are together again.

EPITAPH TO A GOOD MAN

Do nothing today. Say nothing today.
My dear Dan has gently slipped away.
Cast down your eye. Hang down your head.
The love of my life, my soul; is dead.
I must not sorrow, I must not grieve.
But hold myself to myself and silently shout,
Dan is free, free at last, has broken out,
from a prison of a life bound by bonds,
of conscience, faith, duty and sounds,
of children crying, lovers sighing, friends needing.
Now his soul can fly, his spirit can soar,
leaving his body behind, needed no more.

But we who he left, never saying goodbye.
Need to fill in this gap, need to know why,
he had to leave, before we could show,
the love that we felt, the warmth and the glow
of a caring mind, a spirit that cared.
Gave us peace of mind, troubles shared.
Rejoice in his life his deeds and his trust
in all that was good, it will never be lost.
Cry for the need to grieve over what's passed.
Cry for yourself if you feel that you must
But don't cry for him, his burden has gone.
Just treasure his memory, remember his love.

My Mother died about the same time, but the emotions were very different. We had been emotionally separated from each other for most of our lives, although Mother never stopped trying to close the gap. I did write the following poem when she died and ever since my stance as softened. Maybe, I should have been more forgiving.

EPITAPH TO MOTHER

Now she has gone and there is empty space.
The subtle reproach of empty silent rooms.
Her clothes, her jewellery, personal things.
Rest in her room, in silent accusation.

And I must face the guilt,
of all the things I should have done
and never did.

I gave her a poem. She gave me a prayer.
I gave her excuses, she gave me a conscience.
I wrote her such beautiful lines,
letters, full of cheer, full of hope.

She kept every one, read them many times.
I gave her my paintings and she loved them
I gave her everything
except myself.

She could have my duty,
have my presence,
have my belief,
everything except my love.
It was never there to give.

At fourteen my love died
and could not be revived.
No matter how I tried,
prayed and agonized,

The past can never justify the present,
never excuse.
So I give thanks for her later years.
When she found her God
and spiritual peace.
In the company of good friends
and faithful souls.
She is now, where she always wished to be.

This poem comes from my truly desperate times just after I retired. Since I was a teenager I have been fascinated by how people would see my life.

WHAT WILL THEY REMEMBER?

What will they say when I die?
Was I good?
Will they tell it as it was
or as they saw it?
Will they say what I did
to help this world along?
Or say how I failed,
how I went wrong?

Whatever they say,
I will reach the other side,
Glad to go and not afraid.
I will expect nothing,
will get nothing,
will go to nothing.

At least there will be relief
that all is over.
No more need to try,
no more need to live a lie.
I am tired of what masquerades for life.
The hypocrisy of living,
when the memories bite so deep,
and leave the wounds, which never heal.
Never can heal,

because they constantly reopen.
When you never know happiness
then sorrow becomes a friend.
I have so much hurtful guilt,
I no longer wonder why God turns away.
Would be disappointed if it were not so.
I welcome sorrow, welcome guilt, welcome self-disgust.
I know you all.

Recently I have been experimenting with very tight, short, verse, which says a great deal in a few words. This is one such attempt.

REGRET

Last night I dreamt
Of my late wife
Long departed
And I was sad
For all the things that might have been.

This is my final word on anything to do with death; mine or
anyone elses. I am in grave danger (pardon
the pun), of becoming morbid. Mind you,
I wouldn't say 'no' to such a peaceful event!

A GENTLE PASSING

We were climbing the mountain
To the peak bathed in light.
The valley was dark and misty,
With shadows soft and dark,
Pulling me down with gentle persuasion.
She held my hand so tenderly.
She smiled at me and softly mouthed;
I love you, but I must leave you,
And she was young again, beautiful to behold.
She continued upward.
And I?
I turned back to the valley.
to the soft, warm, inviting, dark.
There I joined with other souls,
for eternity!
But my love never faded.

POEMS OF LOVE AND REGRET

I was living and working in Nigeria and conditions were difficult to say the least. On one particularly difficult day, I came home exhausted. My wife met me at the door. She led me to a chair, put a drink in my hand and said, "Tell me all about it." It struck me then and there, how lucky I was to be married to such a wonderful woman, one I most certainly did not deserve. Later that evening the poem that follows slipped into my head, complete. It was the first poem I wrote but many others followed.

JUST BE!

It is enough for me that you are on this earth:
It is enough for me that you look upon this earth and
    smile:
It is enough for me that you laugh and love:
It is enough for me that you love even when hurt:
It is enough for me that even hurt you care for me.

Many expatriate men live alone in Nigeria. Their wives remain at home with children or for other powerful reasons. The men become very lonely and find their solace in drink or female company. Many Nigerian girls are attractive and are fascinated by England and the things that relatively rich men can offer. The results are in many cases, heartbreaking. This next poem was inspired by the sadness I observed on both sides from friends, who despite their best intentions, fell in love.

GOODBYE MY LOVE'

Hold me tight!
Don't let me go.
Squeeze me hard,
so I will know,
that you will grieve,
when I must leave.

Show me your face,
for one last time.
Give me a smile,
let your eyes shine.
Give me a memory,
that will always be mine.

Now I must depart,
but I leave you my life.
We will not meet again.
We will not love again.
I must go back to my
innocent wife.

I think everyone has an aura which can be expressed
as a colour. The next poem expresses my feelings.
It is of course a little bit of whimsy: a confection
for a wife or lover.

COLOURS

Everyone has their own colour.
Yours is blue or cool green,
while I am hot fiery red,
at the other end of the spectrum.
That's how it seems to me,
when I consider our reflections.
You are cool and clear and bright,
sparkling crystal, crisp winters's night.
But me, I catch fire, hotly glow,
moth at a candle, singeing slow.
A shooting star, gone too soon.
Leaving the ashes, waning moon.
I need someone steady to slow down my life.
Add some blue and some green, watercolour wife.
Paint me gently into a picture of calm,
use cooling colours, soft soothing balm.

People, particularly the elderly have so many sad memories of lost loves. This is particularly poignant at Christmas.

THE MISTLETOE

The old man stands alone, erect and still,
silent guard at the sitting room window.
Looking out at a sullen, grey, Christmas,
a road of damp trees, defeated gardens.
In his hand, the mistletoe, green and fresh.
He waits, as he has done for fifty years,
for a secret love, who will never come.
Then, in his mind, she gracefully enters.
He greets her, takes her gently at the waist,
holding the mistletoe, high above her head.
She slowly turns her face up to be kissed;
Her soft trembling lips meet his once again,
the same as she has done each Christmas past.
Slowly, he takes her hand and fits the ring.
Another clinging kiss; a lover's waltz,
round and around, dip'n'down, looking love.
The music stops, she caresses his cheek.
One more kiss, then slowly she fades away.
His memory over for another year,
He celebrates grey Christmas day alone.

This next poem was written when getting to know my first granddaughter, Claire-Lise. This tiny little girl, full of love and trust, full of life and laughter, overwhelmed me.

GRANDCHILD

Tiny kisses on my cheek.
Hugs so tight I cannot speak.
Tiny body pressed to mine.
I love you Grandpa; joy sublime!
Hold her gently less she break.
Caress her softly, there's no mistake.
She's from our child, our family stock.
Favours her Mum. Oh what luck.

'Tell me a story Grandpa,
'bout how you won the war.
'bout lions 'n dragons and things that you saw.
Tell me when you met my Gran.
Was she beautiful like a queen?
The loveliest lady you've ever seen?'

'Yes my lovely. I'll tell you all,
and through your eyes grow very tall.
I'll live my life again through you,
and tell of experience; a guide for you.
No need to make the mistakes I made.
You can win when life's game is played.

It is very difficult for parents when the first boyfriend appears. Certainly the choices our daughters made gave cause for concern. The following poem echoes these concerns but as the reader will see I have changed the context. It was safer that way.

THE GIRLFRIEND

Give the girl a chance Mum!
Extend a friendly hand.
She's better than you think Mum,
though not the type you planned.
She's really very nice Mum,
just like a loving daughter.
The one you never had Mum.
Sharing hopes and joyous laughter.
She'd fill your lonely hours Mum,
Talk 'bout things that interest you.
She'll help you out lots Mum,
sharing all the jobs you do.
She cares for me so much Mum;
but not the same as you.
She satisfies my need Mum,
which you can never do.
Though I love her deeply Mum,
I need the both of you.

I enjoyed writing the next poem. It was easy to write and people's reactions to it have been interesting. Some think that it is rude, offensive even pornographic. Others think it is an attempt at humour, which does not quite succeed. I think that such criticisms are much too precious. The poem was always intended to be a robust, romping statement of one persons love for another. I continue to enjoy it. Every time, I envisage young country boys and girls tumbling in the hay.

FOR THE LOVE OF YOU

For the love of you, I no longer see,
the rosy ripe apples on the tree.
For the love of you, I no longer pluck,
the rich, luscious fruit,
trusting my luck, by gently biting,
the soft tender skin,
fragrant juice glistening down my chin.

Instead:
you fill my every pore
and I am helpless,
overcome; craving more.
Your fragrant breath;
moist shivery kiss;
spirals me down slowly,
to quivering bliss,
overwhelmed.

For the love of you, I no longer look,
at beautiful flowers I used to pick.
For the love of you, I no longer dip,
a trembling hand between the lips;
parting the petals, savouring the pollen,
mimicking the bee to taste the honey
upon my greedy mouth.

Instead:
I feed from your delicious lips;
savouring your essence;
sucking tiny sips,
unable to resist that burst of desire,
at the tilt of your head, the fall of your hair.
The hungry hunter has settled.
Replete.
No longer wanting, no longer needing;
Complete; satisfied.

We have three daughters. We are very proud of them.
There is a love which never diminishes and best of
all it works both ways. Many times in the past, when
in deep depression, it is the thought of our daughters
that has helped turn life around.

REFLECTIONS IN A FOREST POOL

Walking slowly through the summer forest
I stumbled on a tiny pool.
Marooned by the passing stream, it was
crystal mirror clear and oh so cold.
I saw my face reflected there, sad and lined,
with all my failures and losses aging me.

Then a whispering wind gently stirred the surface
and my unhappy face had gone.
I looked again; new faces were reflected there.
Etched across them, love and proud achievement.
Happiness, fond memories, caring laughter.
My first reflection never told a proper story
It gave no credence to my lovely daughters.
They were my success; they were my glory.

And so the picture changed again.
Your face was reflected there, smiling and serene.

I continued walking, leaving the pool behind me.
Which showed a mirror to my soul.
I moved on content with what I had.
No longer needing a verdict on my life.
I am proud of what I have,
I have a wife; she gave me daughters,
And each one is a masterpiece.

The older you become, the more time appears to speed away. Inevitably thoughts turn to the time when everything comes to an end.

NIGHT THOUGHTS!

Soft night, dark night,
warm as the velvet touch
of your skin against mine.
The sensation too much,
for sleep to come.
So I lay and listen as you breathe
and imagine all our futures,
think of all that's past.

One day all this must end,
but please not yet.
Let time stand still
or at least go slow.
There is so much more to do,
so much more to know.
Don't let our idyll end,
let it not be close.

But when the end does finally come,
let's embrace it boldly.
Because it is unknown,
Doesn't mean it must be feared.
But until the day;
come, savour every moment.
Living for today,
may tomorrow never come.

And now, content,
I can stop the wheels within my mind.
Shut down my old man worries,
Ignore my aches and pains.
Down deep in the pillow,
feeling your smooth warmth,
soothing my mind, stroking my senses,
so I can sleep.

Successfully loving someone, for a long time is
magnificently rewarding, but like most good things,
it requires hard work and sacrifice. The golden
rule is that each must put your partner first. It works!

LOVE LIVES

You can't put conditions on love.
Can't say you will,
or you won't.
To be in love is not an act of conscious will,
It just happens.
And when it does,
it consumes you.

To stay in love is something you can decide.
You have a choice,
to stay in love
or not.
Love is a delicate flower, easily withered,
With the creeping paralysis,
of easy familiarity,
of everyday dull
and ordinary things.

Love needs dedicated nurturing,
once the excitement dies,
and loving becomes a duty,
not joyous exploration.
Love needs the freshness that new excitements bring.
Selfless thought for each other,
trying to please,
in new ways.

*I watched a film called 'The Bridges of Madison County'.
I found it deeply moving and I just had to write a poem
about it. It hit me hard because a similar thing happened
to a very close friend of mine. I could only watch
as my friend slowly died a spiritual death.*

THE BRIDGES OF MADISON COUNTY

A story of unlucky lovers,
who never should have met,
and never should have loved,
but could not help themselves.

Chance gave them just four days
of loving bliss.
The pleasure of sinking,
each into the other,
Spirit, mind, and bodies intertwined,
Until the two became one.
Four days from making to breaking!
Then family duties triumphed
And marriage vows were obeyed
The lovers stayed apart.
Keeping their secret until they died.
Never meeting, never speaking, never knowing.
Yet their love remained,
Sealed within their deepest memory.

Perhaps they will meet again
in another life, where they can love again.
She inwardly nursed her unrequited love.
He drank his disappointment every day.
They held their secret to themselves
And so kept their dignity, self respect
and partial peace of mind.

I make no apology for my return to the theme
of growing old and the thoughts that
go through an old man's head.

TIME SLIPS AWAY

Time is slipping from my grasp.
Away from my control.
Like grains of sand slowly leaking
through my anxious fingers.
Precious seconds are wasted,
Lost and gone forever.
No one can foresee
when the seconds will cease to flow.
Time is so precious, though we
allow it drift away.
Unremarked, having no meaning,
never labelled, lost memories.
Those hours that tell of the time,
when I so loved my wife,
my emotion overflowed.
My spirit, taking wing.

We are still together
and no matter what life offers,
we will welcome every moment,
Marking it with a loving bond.
Making sure our children,
say, in years to come, 'Oh Yes, remember?
They were in love together.

*This was really sparked off by memories of my
teenage years. It is a teen poem, simple and direct.
I hope it captures the anxieties of a fifteen year old.*

PHONING YOU

I hold the phone,
I hear it ring.
My heart skips a beat,
perhaps you're in.

Will you speak to me?
What shall I say?
What can I say?
To make you feel as I do now?
You say that you do not care for me.
That another has your heart.
But I still hope to change your mind.
Let's make another start.

Let's give it all another chance.
Try harder still this time.
Perhaps our love can blossom,
into something more sublime.

What shall I say?
What can I say?
To make you feel,
as I do now.

It is 58 years since I first kissed my wife. I still
clearly remember and treasure the memory.
It is something I will never forget.

THE FIRST KISS

If, at the end of my days,
I could keep just one moment,
I would choose, the first time
I kissed you.

I remember,

A young girls trusting, quivering lips
feathering mine, as eyes closed,
fluttering hands gently held
my arms.

I remember

A feeling of wonderment, disbelief
and the helpless feeling overcoming me
that meant I'd lost my heart.

I have held on to that precious instant,
treasuring the memory.
A perfect moment, that started an everlasting love.

The nature of my work meant that I spent long periods alone. This continued after I retired, due to my wife spending each week baby sitting our grandson. It was 100 miles away so she only came home at weekends. The following poem stems from those experiences.

SOLITARY MAN

I am a solitary man
Most of my life is lived inside my head
Imagining problems and opportunities
to be exploited in a clever way.
Great books to be written, honours to flow.
Becoming rich and comfortable, serene of mind.
a winner, a champion.
The world's greatest philanthropist.
A wise man full of sage advice.
Beautiful women at my feet, hoping for a glance.
but even in this wonderful world
there is only one companion that I crave
and that is you my love.

But life must be lived outside my head
where life is harder and I am not successful.
For I am an ordinary, solitary man,
nothing special, nothing grand.
I have a life that's average, mostly bland.
But there is something special
that saves me from the norm
and that is you my love and I rejoice.
I bless the fates that gave me you
someone I never deserved and who has filled my life
with pleasures, treasures and measures of
wisdom and of love.

I have supped from the cup of happiness many
times and in the end I craved for it.

ADDICTION

My love for you is like a drug,
A habit, which I never can deny.
A craving for you to show me
just how much you love me.
A compulsion
and I never get enough.

I just need to hear you love me.
To soothe my doubting mind.
And when I do not get my daily dose
I slowly wither and die,
from my imagined rejection.

This was one of the Christmas poems but I feel that it fits better in this section. This particular year I found great difficulty in finding a suitable subject and voice. However, I did find the poem that follows. It was probably inspired by thoughts of Peter Pan and Never Never Land.

THE OTHER SIDE OF MAYBE

There is a place the other side of maybe;
A land of dreams and wishes.
Where dreams come true and love can grow,
Where the weather's warm and life goes slow.
Where pains and worries never exist,
And troubles fade like will o' wisps.
You and I can just drift away.
Go to this land where we can stay.
All you must do is hold my hand.
Close your eyes, let your mind expand,
And you will find you are in that land,
Where dreams come true, just as we planned.
Because we have grown old as one,
Fought the winters, shared the sun,
Learned how to love, how to cry.
We can live there you and I.
We can stay there 'til we die
And even then not be apart.
For this is a place which is in the heart.
A land where logic can never start,
To reason away our hopes and wishes.
A land of joy, a land of riches,
A land of the mind, for you for me.
Where we can let our reality be.

This following poem is just a figment of my imagination. However it is inspired by real life events in the Philippines, where girls, desperately poor, live in hope of a better life.

THE TRIALS OF LOVE

I gave you my heart
You tore it apart
Threw back the pieces
Laughing at me.
Walking away
You 'killed me' that day.
Now I am grieving
The loss of a lover:
And I can't accept
It's really all over
Before it began.

A very good friend of mine, whose opinion I deeply respect, described the next poem as 'over the top'! I disagree! When you are truly in love logical, sensible thought has no place and we struggle to find suitable words to describe our feelings. What do you think?

SOLITARY THOUGHTS OF YOU

When I think of you,
all the memories,
Distil,
into one single drop,
of happiness.

When I look at you,
the lines of your face,
overwhelm me
and I fill up,
with emotion.

When my arms hold you,
the sensation,
is much more than
I can bear without,
crying out.

POEMS TO MAKE YOU SMILE

The following was inspired by the confessions of friend of mine during a beer filled 'after work' session in Nigeria. He had lived alone too long.

AFRICAN GIRL

Brown skin, smooth skin, just like silk.
Brown skin, soft skin, chocolate milk.
Colour rich velvet; warm to the feel.
Pleasure to see; almost not real.

Hourglass shape; dark and inviting.
Soft parted lips, too exciting.
Moist steamy breath, whenever I look.
Shortage of breath, brain starts to cook.

Too perfect to hold; cannot desist.
Trouble to love; pain to resist.
This girl's obsession, like white powder drug.
Compelled to be with her; gives heart strings a tug.

Not really mine; brains in a whirl.
Too old to attract such a young girl.
Walk away now; you never have met.
Get on with your life; but never forget

*For many years, for those living and working in Ikeja,
Lagos, the Airport Hotel was the only place to stay,
to drink and to gamble (it had a casino). It was a rough
'down at heel' place but the alternatives were even less
attractive. If you went to the Airport Hotel you had
to run the gauntlet of the working girls.*

YOUNG GIRL

'Do you have a problem?' the young girl said.
'Do you always stare at ladies in red?
I know my dress is brief and scarlet,
but that doesn't mean that I'm a harlot.
Even tho' my neckline is much too low,
don't think about, what I might show.
You can see quite plain, my dress is split,
I don't like how your eyes are lit.
Even though, you can see my thigh,
you've got your hopes up, far too high.
But: if you persist:
make your desires so plain.
Then I'm forced to agree.
Your place or mine?'

I really enjoyed writing the following poem. It started life as an email joke but I think it works better as a poem.

THE VICAR

Settling in the old armchair,
smiling gently at my guest.
Sipping malt, easing deeper,
after dinner rest.
It's time to tell a story,
a chronicle of jest.
A funny one, listen well,
laugh and be impressed!

Met my vicar the other day,
stopped him for a chat.
'How are you vicar, keeping well?'
I always ask him that!
He always says,
'Thank you my son,
God bless your sentiment,
God bless you, your wife and kids.'
'I see you are intent
in getting quickly to the pub.
It is my aim as well.
I need a drink quite badly,
tho' my way be straight to hell!
The trouble is, I'm forced to walk,
instead of cycling over.
My poor feet are killing me.
causing me to suffer.'
'Someone stole my bicycle,
my old sentimental pride.

The parish has a thief or two,
it wounds me deep inside.
What can I do, I ask myself,
just how to find the thief?
I'm at my wits end,
my trouble is rotting my belief.'

'Don't worry vicar', I piped up.
'I have a bright idea.
Wait until next Sunday.
Make your sermon strong and clear.
Preach the Ten Commandments.
"thou shalt not steal; its wrong!
God will judge all sinners,
retribution hard and long!'

'Watch the congregation.
Be sure look straight into their eyes.
Spot who looks uncomfortable,
whose temperature's too high.
That will give away your thief,
their conscience in a mess.'
'I'll give it a try' the vicar said:
'lets drink to my success.'

A week went by and once again;
on my way to get a drink.
The vicar passes on his old bike.
What am I to think?
'I see you were successful then,
your sermon did the trick?'
'Yes' he said. 'I preached the Ten Commandments,
fiery, full and strong.
Made sure I told them "thou shalt not"
Taught them right from wrong!'

But when I got to where it's wrong
"to covet thy neighbours' wife".
I knew I was more sinner than sinned against
Oh sorry, sorry life!
Nothing certain, nothing sure;
so please don't take the Michael.
At last I knew where I had left,
my old and trusty cycle.'

This next poem is the result of too much time on my own daydreaming in front of the computer.

TAKING A SHOWER

Took a shower, slipped on the soap!
Feet in the air, grabbed for the rope,
that holds up the curtain: that comes down too.
Try to get up, slip once again.
Slide on the floor, run away train!
Into the door, smash through with ease.
Straight down the stairs, land in a heap.
Feels like bones broken, better call help!

Wife comes by. 'I haven't time now,
Mum's coming round, she's teaching me how,
she dealt with me Dad, when just like you,
he played SAS, or baling out crew.
Pick yourself up! Stop making a mess.
Stop fooling around; being a pest.'

Crawl back upstairs, battered and worn.
Step in the shower, carefully turn,
to put on the tap.
Tread on the soap! Arse over tip!
Back down the stairs, back in a heap.
There's really no hope for someone like me.
A hopeless case, I'm sure you agree.

It is surprising how the mind wanders when you lie awake in the early hours. I wrote this piece of nonsensical whimsy at three in the morning.

NIGHT TIME IN THE SAUNA

Lying in bed,
at three in the morning,
trying to sleep,
and cuddling your naked body;
I am inclined to think,
that you should turn over,
smile and kiss me,
very hard and,
insist on making love.
Then we would be joined,
together as one.
Never to come apart,
until we die.
Of course,
the reality is,
that you already said,
you were not in the mood,
and now being asleep,
you don't care.
On top of that,
the heat from your body,
is so great,
that it's like a sauna,
under these sheets,
and I am covered in sweat.
This does nothing for sexual desire
and not a lot for peace of mind.

This next poem describes a sort of 'ménage a quatres'.
It is just another little bit of idle time nonsense.

ROUNDABOUT LOVE!

James loves Jane,
But Jane loves John,
Which is difficult.
Particularly since;
John loves Julia;
to distraction!
Sadly however;
Julia loves James;
Who....of course!!!

*This is the result of an idle moment and thinking
about the 'Politics' show on television.*

THOUGHTS OF
A SUCCESSFUL POLITICIAN!

This is the beginning of the end!
Or is it the end of the beginning?
Give me a clue!
What should I do?
Just when I thought the issue was known;
Something happened!
What I thought that I knew:
Was totally wrong!
My confidence blown,
There was nothing to do,
But go back to bed.
Stuff my ears and cover my head!
When I wake up, if the world's still around,
I'll start up again feeling safe; feeling sound!
Whatever it was, wherever it went,
It's no longer there.
Wonder what the worry was for?

After a long and happy marriage I can say, without fear of contradiction, that the only way to approach sex is with an exaggerated sense of humour and with the grumpy switch turned firmly off.

RECONSIDER MY DEAR!

The embarrassing silence,
when the question was asked,
was a sign that all was not well.
All I asked was if we could try it,
I needed to ring my bell!
But the way that you lay there,
clenching your thighs,
pretending your mind was elsewhere.
Made it clear to my bell,
There was none to be had.
My ambitions were all shot to hell.

I want you to take a fresh look my dear.
Consider the medicinal need.
It's no more than taking a tablet or two.
I have to deposit my seed.
Think through the options again my love.
Look at the problem once more.
Perhaps we could employ a suitable girl,
who fancies a suitable fee.
She could remove the burden from you
and give satisfaction to me.

So lets try to solve this difference of view.
Lets make a bedroom of peace.
I won't ask if we can do it once more.
You don't give me the tease.
Come to bed in less than your best.
Leave off the cream and the scent.
Give your soft silky nighties a rest.
Flatten your chest, behave like a gent.

I'll come to bed handcuffed and gagged,
Having spent the evening in church.
I'll blindfold my eyes and stuff up my ears
and be sure to be well out of reach.
I will lie on the bed as stiff as a board
Holding the book and the cross
Ready to reject the temptation of flesh
Accepting my feelings of loss.

I was in America visiting my grandchildren. I had just finished reading my book. I was looking for something to do. Watching American television had as much appeal as going for a walk in the rain. It was raining! I was bored. Then I saw my granddaughters' shoes, odd coloured and undone and the following poem was born.

BLACK LACES

Walking down the street
Not looking,
just staring at my feet.
New shoes, bright shiny brown.
Extra thick soles, sturdy black laces.
Black laces! Black laces!
On a shiny brown shoe!
That's not right! That never will do!
Immediate action! Take them out now!
Tuck them away, continue to walk.
Shiny brown shoes slip up and down,
then start to talk!
Clickety clack, clackety click,
Clogs on the pavement clickety clack!
Trip over the curb, flat on my back.
Broken my leg, lost my new shoes,
But still got my laces,
they're black, yes they're black.

Several of my friends are called Harry. One of them
used to drive me crazy with his non-stop talking.
This small poem is just a flight of fancy. By the way,
'me lud' is a corruption of 'my lord' and is
a term used to address a judge.

THE TROUBLE WITH HARRY

The trouble with Harry,
My friend Harry,
Is he never shuts up when he should!
I told him about it.
He said that he would!
But he didn't, he couldn't,
So I shot him, me lud!

*We have friends who used to live in Trinidad. We stayed
with them several times and always had a good time. Yvonne
and Clive were always very hospitable and we spent many
relaxing rum filled evenings with them on their patio, gazing
out at the tropical night. The next three poems are very
much 'tongue in cheek'. I should explain that both Yvonne
and Clive came from the Birmingham area and we originally
met them in Nigeria when we were all much younger.
Everyone would comment on 'how alike' Yvonne and my
wife were. 'They must be sisters'. They could have been but
they weren't. I was never surprised therefore that I found it
easy to write about Yvonne and Clive.*

VISITING TRINIDAD

Do you remember?
Last February it was!
Sitting on the patio, drinking,
Situation normal!
Write me a poem you said.
'Specially for me, your friend!
Well what should I write?
What did you want?
What kind sort of a tome?
There was never a clue.
Was it just a few lines,
or a sonnet or two?
An epic of love?
Ah but then Clive might sue!
Well the first thing that came to my fevered brow:
Was:

BLOND BRUMMIE BELLE!

Well here's to you my Blond Brummie Belle!
A toast!
A drink to a woman I trust.
To the kind-hearted way you behave.
To that curly blond smile
with those crinkly eyes,
And the look that's both knowing and wise
A toast to my lovely Birmingham Belle!
To the way the men hover around.
Trying to impress, say something profound,
Hoping to take her feet off the ground.
Some of them say, with hand upon heart,
Head tilted back, eyes raised firmly on high
That for the sake of one kiss,
from her heavenly lips,
They'd lie down and happily die.
So nothing but praise for my Birmingham Belle
As she looks up from under her brows,
And gives them a smile that's nothing but wry,
As she walks right away with a smile and a sigh,
Leaving the victim quite ready to die.
And wily old Clive who's spotted it all!
Knows bloody well what she's done.
Knows very well she's only for him.
Thank God for his blond Brummie Belle!

YVONNE

Yvonne, Yvonne, you are driving me mad!
For God's sake, God's sake! Do something bad!
With me!
I beg you, stop being, so bloody nice!
Find your own personal Devil
Please practice a personal vice.
A big one! With me!
I'm very serious now!
You have to learn how!
To be hedonistic, masochistic, sadadistic even ballalistick
Futuristick, parasitic, or even just manic.
How about crazy? Crazy?
Sure, crazy for me!

But you won't will you? You never will.
Jolly old Clive, has you under his spell
And you're ever so good and who would blame YOU?
I would as I punch this wall.
I would blame you!

BRIDGE IN TRINIDAD

Four 'Trini' ladies, playing bridge in the nude!
One said 'no bid' the other 'you're rude
Bidding no bid, while scratching your boob.'
'When you've nothing to hide! Oh yes! One spade!'
The third one said 'I can feel a lump, I'm so overweight,
I must slim down. Ok just one more of your tarts!
Oh and by the way, I'll bid two hearts.
Oh what shall I bid said the fourth with a sigh.
Which raised up her bosom from off of her thigh.
The problem I have is who has the knave?
And I've hair under my arms, d'you think I should shave?
I fear if I bid we shall fall with a bump
Oh bugger it now I'll go two no trump.

The first little lady said: 'Oh lets forget about bridge,
Lets just go for a swim instead!
So just as they were,
that's just what they did.

CONTEMPORARY LIFE

Too often Senior Managers are 'jobs worth' individuals
who have spent their working lives following the rules,
sucking up to all their superiors and making sure that
none of their subordinates ever present a threat to
their own position. These mediocre management
hacks never give any thought to the greater
good of the company and its staff.

THE JOB

There are many ways to be an ass.
Ensure proceedings descend to farce.
My Boss is a master of the foul up:
A wizard of screw up, cock up, shut up.
Don't talk about it; it never took place.
Blame somebody else, just save your fat face.
Carefully planned for maximum chaos.
The good of the company, just don't fail us.
Sacrificial goat, surplus requirement.
Sorry you must go. Severance payment.
More pitying looks than pounds in the bank.
What to do next. "May I be frank?
You're over qualified here, fifty too old,
We're in need of young men, you don't fit the mould."

So what's to be done, just how do you live?
Preserve self-respect, prove you're alive.
Why, start your own business, be your own boss.
Do whatever you like and don't give a toss.
Let all those stuffed shirts play the company game.
  Watch the fear in their eyes, "Who takes the blame?"

Work hard for yourself; give it all you've got.
What ever you earn, you've got the lot.
Expand when you can, a worker or two,
Look after them well; see how they do,
when given the chance to grow with the task.
"You took a risk! Why didn't you ask?
You have killed any hope of a future with us.
I trust you'll leave now without any fuss."

Trying to meet the demands of a difficult job that requires far more than regular hours, with little or no support and ever increasing demands from superiors is stressful anywhere. In the environment of Lagos Nigeria it became impossible.

STRESS

I perch on a tension rope.
Tight and taut, can hardly cope,
with the strains of a life;
twanging and keening, razors edge.
Will I break? I know I might.
Hold it! Hold it in! I'd like to fight,
all those who stand in the way.
Somebody! Somebody's got to pay!
Lonely bitterness is my comfort.
Cynical sympathy easily found
from such as you: smug superiority.
What do you say? How do you know?
You haven't been there, suffered the blow.
Blow after blow, life beating me down.
A plot by you bastards who just want to own,
my life and my soul and all I possess.
And you want to know about my distress?
Go away now; leave me alone!
Get out of my life! Haven't I shown?
I'm all in control!
So what are those screams?
Am I doing that?
It's not what it seems.

I know exactly what it is like to be alone.
Wherever you are, whatever you are doing there
is a huge void in your life. Nothing you can
do can assuage these feelings.

ALONE

Most of the time
you are not aware.
You can ignore the fact
there's no one there.
But then you realise
you are quite alone,
and you cannot fill
the increasing space.
The walls drift away;
you are on your own.
You rush around
as if it were a race,
to fill the minutes, hours, days.
Time crawls along
so slowly,
Leaving the slimy trail of its passing.

Your constant companion is the radio,
A voice to say hullo, how are you?
To say there are others,
out there, doing things.
Not staying in,
looking at receding walls.
Its time to eat,
chew every mouthful slowly;

Taking time.
The postman comes,
another important event.
Hope for something,
from someone who knows you,
who cares.
There is nothing today,
perhaps tomorrow.

Soon after I retired I was in a very dark place, not at all sure of my own self worth. Issues and events as dark as my own moods were well suited to my frame of mind. I joined a creative writing class in an effort to at least focus some of my thoughts. Then, I read an account of a woman's violent rape at the hands of a drunken husband. This is commonplace in many parts of the world, but this was closer to home. It set off a train of thought which resulted in the following poem. I apologise to anyone with a sensitive disposition.

GOD HELP ME

He raped me! Oh God I feel unclean.
So ashamed, so dirty, so; obscene.
Where's the justice? What does life mean?
How could he do it, strong to my weak?
How does he see me, some kind of freak?
Yet he's my husband, love, honour, cherish.
He forgets about that; just use 'til I perish.
He comes from the pub, falling down drunk,
grabbing at me, squeezing each chunk
of a body that's bruised, hurt by the strain
of just being used to banish his pain.
There's nowhere to go; it's pointless to run.
I would kill myself now, were it not for my son.
Soon he'll be big, protect me by force.
Give me the strength to seek a divorce.
Then we'll be happy; we can wait until then.
Oh my God! He's waking again.

Within the Creative Writing Class there were many arguments about the previous poem. They ranged from: 'as a man you have no right to even attempt to write about such a subject' all the way up to 'it's very good but much too raw and much too brutal'. The most telling comment was 'it has promise, you should rewrite it and tone it down a little'. Well I went away and rewrote it! The result is below! I titled it:

A KIND OF LOVE

He raped me!
Oh God I feel unclean.
I feel so guilty; so obscene!
Why would he hurt me?
Why would he force me?
Where came the anger,
the hate 'stead of love?
Did I provoke him
So he must take,
what he could have?
I hate him!
I love him!

I want to crawl away and die.
I want to wash him out of me.
No, that would be a lie!
There he sleeps, beside me.
He doesn't see my tears.
He doesn't know my anger,
my disgust; my body's pain.
He doesn't care about my fears,
he will do it all again,
unless I leave him now.
I love him!
I hate him!

Let me wash away and soothe away,
the marks of his assault.
Let me creep away and hide away,
the signs of my body's guilt.
Let me have the strength to carry on.
to be a wife to him,
I need to be a lover,
I need to give my heart.
This is what it has to be.
Can I make him see?
Oh Mother, Mother! Please help me!

*Perversely, my writing class decided that the poem
was just too soft and did not reflect the true feelings
of the victim. I should try to express more of the
anger the victim feels. I found that I could not leave
the subject without trying once more. It was about
this time that I also read a most moving story that
featured an abused wife. The two issues came together
and the following poem was written. It is well outside
my normal thoughts of what poetry should be and
I almost did not include it. One result of this poetry
was that it made me thoroughly ashamed of
the injustices, indignities and insensitivity men
display toward women. This is my attempt to
show some of the anger women rightfully feel.*

A KIND OF MARRIAGE

Heavy, beery, body,
crushing, stamping,
kill the insect dead.
Spearing, stabbing,
drowning in blood,
push down his head.
Bleed on the creep,
'til the fat slug floats,
push him away;
push him down.
Him, him, I hate the prick.
Good, good,
I'm gonna be sick.

I stood in front of that priest
and said that I do.
Just for this beast.
I must have been blind,
To all that he said.
Did I ever love him?
Now I wish he were dead.
Oh God that one hurt!
Up into my womb!

If you keep thrusting like that,
It'll be me in my tomb.
'Are you far enough in?
Are your balls up as well?'

'Well I'm floating above
this ridiculous scene,
You're just a piston and pump.'
With stupid white buttocks,
Pounding and thumping,
Like some anaemic boiled ham,
White and greasy,
waiting to be sliced for family lunch.

The curtains need cleaning,
where his dirty hands,
have pulled them together.
But, let them be open.
Let everyone see, what he is doing to me.
Let's entertain the curtain peepers!

My bruises are a lovely shade of black.
They compliment my eye!
but I can still see.
It hurts inside to walk.
I wish I could catch something, puss filled

and pass it on to him.
I should feel ashamed, I don't.
I feel proud to have swallowed him up,
drained off his seed.
But, never, never, can I do it again!

So He must go or I must go.
Better be him.
I'll wait until he sleeps
and I'll fuck him instead!
but I'll use a knife not a prick.
Plunge it in, again and again
'till the blood runs deep and thick.
I will go down and I will drown,
but he will become the violated one.
He will never understand.

*I was deeply moved by the Warrington bomb, which
had been placed by the IRA. It caused so much death;
destruction and heartbreak yet achieved nothing. There
are those who will never learn. The next poem records
my feelings about such mindless slaughter.*

NEVER FORGET

Sean obeyed the voice,
inside his head,
hammering home, the whispered orders,
given by the shadowy face, with silvery hair.

Drive with sense now!
At the target, park with care.
Set the fuse, lock the van,
get out of there!

Walk away slow.
Do not look back.
Round the corner, hop a bus.
You have twenty minutes,
no need to rush.

Tony walking with his Dad.
Ten years old and very proud.
Having a chat, man to man.
What he would buy for his Mum.
Tomorrow's her birthday;
His own soon to come.
So good to look forward,
so much to be done.

"For the glory of the Cause!
Kill the English scum!
Send the buggers to Kingdom Come!
Here's to poor Will, crazy John.
One in the Maze, one long gone!"

Sean, an Irish volunteer,
brave and proud, with never a fear,
strolled away.

No room for doubt! Patriotic duty done!
He was feeling fine!
He left a bomb, fused and ready,
Counting down its victim's time.

Tony was pleased with his present,
couldn't wait to see his Mum.
Give her the gift and see her smile.
Hug him to her, thank you Son.
You've made me so happy,
I love you so much, you and your Dad.
I'll treasure it always!
Best present I've ever had.

Tony talked soccer with his Dad.
About his team, the position he played.
He was a striker, good for his age.
He had a match today, his first in the league.
Hand in hand, absorbed in each other;
They passed the van, oblivious.

The bomb exploded!
Too soon! Too early by far!
Catching the patriot.
First to the abattoir!
Two yards on, fatally wounding
the boy called Tony.

They lay with the others,
Hearing, helpless, hopeless, screams.
Feeling the bullet rubble, the dagger glass.

All around, burnt, blackened blood,
the glistening raw of inside flesh.
The hurt of a Nation on display.
Television to dissect,
Politicians to sanitise and tuck away.

Tony; small and young,
trails his blood across the lake of glistening glass,
to where the Patriot lays.
Tenderly he cradles his head.
He thinks it is his Dad;
this moaning, bloody mess.
Gently he shakes his shoulder.
"Come on Dad! Let's go home!
I've got to play this afternoon.
We'll be so late!
I want my Mum!"

Blood to blood!
Commitment cradled by innocence.
The young lad dies,
holding the dead bomber in his lap.
A cameraman takes a moving, prize winning shot.
For twenty four hours the world grieves,
from it's armchair.

Oblivious the battle goes on.
Another Irish volunteer steps up,
Full of belief, full of pride, wanting to serve.
And an English school picks another striker.

"DON'T TALK TO ME OF GOD!"

There he stood on the front door step.
Full of good intentions, washing me with his words.
Explaining his faith and why I should join.
Honouring his God and cementing his belief.
It was too much!

"Don't talk to me of God young man!

I'm too old, too tired, too angry at my life.
Years of effort; no reward.
Wasted talent; wasted hopes.
I was a bright young man, full of belief
That life was fair and life was good.
I lost all that."

"Don't talk to me of God young man!

Ambition died a slow and bitter death.
Leaving behind an empty shell, squeezed dry of hope.
Beaten to submission, ceasing to try!
I watched my friends, and enemies too,
Enjoy the lucky chance.
Rise to the top and there they stayed,
future secure, life safe, insured from any pain.
They will never know that falling off feeling,
from the ladder of success.
'You can climb again', they say;' you can reach the top!
Look it's so easy, never look down, never stop!

But that ladder is built from other people's dreams!
As you grow, as you climb, so you destroy.
Others are left to sink or swim, perhaps to drown.
Never stop, ever on up, never look down!

"Don't talk to me of God young man

If you do look down, do give a helping hand:
Then you never reach the top. Just down you go
And have to start the climb again.
So you never reach your goal.
Are never secure, never at ease, can never stop to rest.
So you ask yourself, 'why am I different?
Why didn't I climb with ease?
And then you realise! You are just the same,
sometimes better than the rest!
It's just the game of chance called life.
Which dealt you a losing hand."

Gods lottery!

"So don't talk to me of God young man."

"You love someone with all your soul,
and think it is returned.
You ignore the tiny seeds of doubt.
Until one day, it hits you, a blow below the belt.
She doesn't love you! Perhaps she never has.
Has always lived in her own private island,
Her own very secret place!

She will not leave it, to join with you.
You wonder why she stays and then it dawns.
She is trapped the same as you, no choice but
to stay together, in watchful truce".

"So don't talk to me of God young man."

And yet this young man is right. I need a God.
To save this empty life.
To let me start to believe again.
To try once more to climb.
But most of all to find the love, I allowed to slip away.
To nurture it and nourish it in my advancing years.

"So talk to me of God young man!
Tell me all you know!
And I will listen, listen, listen.
To every golden word.
And hope that your Saviour will also talk to me.
Guide me on my way.
To climb again, and fight again, secure in what I do.
So talk to me of God young man."

The next poem was inspired by an article in the newspaper about teenage prostitution.

THE CASUALTY

She stands on the corner, wet, cold and scared.
Just fifteen years old and already scarred.
Hoping some man will stop and will fancy,
her blond youth, and vulnerability.

She's run away, couldn't bear to stay home.
Now afraid of her pimp, who takes all she earns.
Beats her about to keep her in line.
She spends her money on drugs and on fines.

A car pulls up, and a window goes down.
She sways over, legs too thin, heels too high.
And fingers crossed, leans forward, breasts on view,
recites her menu to a guilty man.

'It's twenty for oral. Thirty for sex.
Full sexual service is forty or more.
Depends what you want, how long you take
Let me climb in please, open the door.

Back of the car? That's just fine for me.
Drive down there, it's quiet. No one will see.
Pay me now please darlin, then we can start.
Gently now big boy, I'm not yer' ordinary tart.

Why do I do it? Well a girl's gotta live.
It pays more than the factory and some punters are nice.
I want me own flat when I've saved up enough.
Somewhere, nice and quiet, nothin' too rough.

I want a job as a nurse fer handicapped kids.
Get married perhaps, have some of me own.
I'd luv' em to death even after they've grown.
Fer now though it's just beautiful dreams.

Now I've got me work to do
selling the punters a shag.
Oh God it's so cold, lend me a drag.
One just for now, one after I've done.

'You're a nice looker! Come on my love.
You've been driving' around' searching for me?
Do you want good time?
Do you like what you see?

The wars in Iraq and Afghanistan have meant that many times there are poignant scenes as the dead soldiers are brought home.

WHY?

The tear on the old man's face,
like rain on a glossy rose leaf,
sparkled in the weak grey light.
He stood to attention,
holding the hand,
Of a small girl, fair hair awry,
rubbing tearful eyes
with grubby hand.

Their hero gone,
his life and reason has wrenched away.
Even the trees moved quietly, bowing their leaves,
Dripping rain on silent heads.
Every one trod a slow motion dance of mourning,
Wanting to speak but afraid to break the spell.

He was a good man, a caring man, a loving man.
He died an unjust, lonely death, far away.
I see the sorrow, see the pain and have to ask:
where is my faith now?

All the coffins that return to the United Kingdom
are placed in hearses and slow marched, with great
ceremony, through the streets of Royal Wootton Bassett.
Unfailingly the townspeople turn out
to pay their solemn respects.

THE COFFINS KEEP COMING

Day after day, the coffins keep coming!
With flags, carefully draped.
The bugle sounds its mournful dirge
As guards, slow and stately,
Place the coffin in the shiny hearse.
Slowly the cortege moves off,
Silent but for the slow drum beat.
In front the man in the dark suit and top hat
Twirls his ceremonial baton.

The town's people stand in respectful crowds.
Heads bowed, a silent tribute to dead heroes.
Expressing their sorrow, their gratitude.
Soldiers ultimate duty done, are returning home.
In London, a politician utters a few meaningless words,
    in front of cameras, searching for news.
listened to by people who only half care.
He is oblivious to how easy it is to be brave and right,
when thousands of miles from the conflict.

We sometimes forget that our soldiers are first and foremost human beings who sometimes find a real conflict between their humanity and their duty.

A SOLDIERS TALE

He sat in the corner, legs splayed.
Face striped with camouflage paint,
He was very young;
But his eyes were a thousand years old,
staring straight ahead.
He told me he had watched his friend go down
and now his friend was dead.
I could not face that stare,
so quietly crept away;
hoping to see him again,
on a better, happier, day.

He went out again,
another foot patrol, part of his platoon,
patrolling that empty village,
with a courage raw and simple.
Covering his buddies' backs,
shooting at black clad anonymous figures.

That day, he finally saw his enemy,
up close and personal;
looked into fanatical eyes,
full of hatred and murderous intent.
He couldn't pull the trigger,
couldn't shoot the man.
His buddy fired, the man died,
they moved on.
Later; when they stood down,
he faced his private devils alone.

*Expatriate life, in Nigeria, placed a strain on marriages.
It either made them or broke them. One of the main
reasons for many marriages breaking was the voluntary
or enforced absence of the wife. Not all wives
forgave adultery and I knew several very unhappy
men who bitterly regretted what they had done.*

HE WAS LONELY

He was lonely and the girl was there.
Available, willing and so attractive.
Listening to every word he said.
Filling the spaces in his empty home.
So when they fell into the family bed,
It seemed so right, so natural:
But it wasn't! She had her own needs.
While he: thought he was in love again.
As the memory of his wife slowly faded.

Later, mortified and ashamed he realised,
He had betrayed his wife, his family!
Betrayed the love he had for her.
Dare not declare he loved them,
Without sounding so false, so selfish.
All he could do was say,
'Sorry, so sorry for my weakness.
She was there and you were not!

One of the most difficult tasks in ife
is to bring up your children.
No matter how hard you try, mistakes
are made. This poem
refers to one of the worst mistakes
we made as parents,
albeit with the best of intentions.
We sent our youngest
daughter to boarding school and she
hated it. Her older sisters
had no such problems. Our options
were limited so perhaps
that is why we never properly listened to her.
It is something we are now, profoundly sorry about.

WE ALL DESERVE FORGIVENESS

My Mum and Dad, they messed me up
With all their fights, tears and separations,
and me no place to go.
Later:
No matter how I tried, I couldn't forget.
I couldn't forgive.
I couldn't stop loving.
I couldn't be free,
and it tore me apart.

I swore,
I would never do the same to my kids!
We tried so hard, my wife and I.
Our life didn't go to plan,
Other problems intervened.
So we sacrificed all, for the sake of our kids.
Watched them advance and succeed.
Thinking they were happy,
that all was well.

It was a shock to find,
Our youngest felt so wounded,
So distressed, so betrayed!
Abandoned too young at school
with no comfort of home.
She could never forget,
She could never forgive,
But despite everything,
she never stopped loving.

How did we go wrong?
We did what we could,
The best we could do.
It cost us; heartbreak and pain,
But it was the only solution.
She believes we should have tried harder.
Showed more love at the time.
We did, we did, we tried so hard,
Yet we failed and must live with the guilt.

Perhaps that's what my Mum and Dad tried to do.
Their best as they could see it.
Perhaps I should say sorry to my Mum and Dad
Although, long since dead.
For the wasted years, the thoughtless smears,
the hurt, the guilt, the careless abandonment.
My Dad fought back with an angry resentment,
until illness brought weary defeat.
My Mum tried to find peace, forgiveness in God.
Now I think perhaps: perhaps: my Mum was right.

WHIMSICAL THOUGHTS

All of us have at some time or another been jolted
awake by a bad dream or a half heard noise.

DREAMS

Middle night wakening;
jolt by bad dream.
Dark shadowed room,
not what it seems.
Heart pounding hard;
cold sweat on brow!
Get out of bed.
Black, moving night!.
A whisper of movement,
descend into fright.
Check no one is there, turn on the light.
Back to sleep now, everything's right.

I had this image in my head of a voluptuous young woman, with long black hair wearing a bright red evening dress. She is seated, elbows on the dining table and is devouring a tomato with sharp pointed teeth.

IT'S MY SUPPER

She held it, in her hand,
rich, red and ripe.
Such indulgent, voluptuous, fruitfulness.
Shiny- hard, red veined,
a positive statement underlined.
She looked at me and smiled,
lazy possession in her eyes.
Her small, nipping-white teeth,
peeping-perfect from her licking lips.

'Its my supper' she said,
poking her finger into the join,
And with that,
she put the shiny red bulb to her greedy lips,
and began to suck;
on a tightly stretched skin,
shining more brightly than before.

She sucked it in, plopped it out,
a study; in thoughtful satisfaction.
'It's my satisfying supper' she said,
and resumed the suck.
Fidgeting; twisting the fruit,
to taste more of what she wanted.
Stretching the skin.
Then, tiring of what she did,
she began to bite.

Watching, the shiny, tightly stretched skin:
giving way, suddenly bursting,
as bleached bone, snow white, teeth
sunk in.
Juice spurting; she swallowed,
staining her cheeks and breast.
'It was my supper' she said.

All that was left, were stains of it's passing,
And scary memories of her pointed, perfect, teeth.

*My wife and daughters all read the Vampire novels
and I am constantly having images brought to
my attention. I am not a fan, but on the other
hand if you can't beat 'em, join 'em.*

VAMPIRE

The spider web, clinging, whispers of the night,
blanket and protect me.
Others cannot see me when the goddess
drives out the light and I am safe.

Neither can you see me, yet you kiss my lips,
touching my bashful scars.
You touch angry, ruined, flesh, yet,
I am beautiful within your mind.

I hold you, bending your soft body,
in perfidious tenderness.
You cannot see my hands begin to clench;
urgent mouth begin to drip.

The rich ripeness of your rosy blood,
Will bleed from your trusting soul.
You will not die my love, just warmly fade,
as your life flows into mine.

Every man I know, has at some time or another,
gazed at a beautiful woman silhouetted
in a doorway with the sun shining through
her dress and has wondered..

DAYDREAMS FOR A BEAUTY!

I saw you standing in the doorway

And the sunlight shone through your dress

Silhouetting your figure against the light.

I could not help but think: life is unfair

That you keep your beauty for one man only;

While the rest of us yearn, for what might have been.

Seven years ago I was diagnosed with Cancer. I spent quite a long time in treatment before ultimately recovering. What follows reflects the way I dealt with the problem. I bleached my hair blond, which looked silly but every time I looked in the mirror it reminded me to never give up.

UPSIDE, DOWNSIDE. (ON HEARING I HAD CANCER.)

Say it in the morning. Say it in the evening.
Say it clear. Say it loud,
Say it at the looking glass.
Say it every day,
don't let a moment pass.

I'm better than this, stronger than this
Talk to God and say
If you won't give me decent luck
I'll make it myself. Anyway!

I know I don't deserve my fate,
And I will fight to win.
I'll bloody well show the lot of you,
From now my life will be my own.

I have the will, I have the knowledge.
I have strength of mind and spirit.
I have friends that matter, friends that care.
And above all that, I am loved in prayer.

And when all is said, all is done!
I'll go out and show them
Turn life around, upside down, inside out.
Move right on, remove all doubt.

It's all about being in hospital with
a Tracheotomy tube.
If you don't know what that is, you are lucky.
So don't worry about it!

THE ACCIDENT

It is your Birthday!
As you lie in that hospital bed,
Why not watch TV they said!
I did! Then I,

Turned over in bed!
The sound went off!
Rolled on the remote,
The TV went off!
I coughed too hard,
The speech cap blew off!

Tried to catch it,
My drip pulled off!
Hit the button,
The beep went off
The nurse takes off!

Oh hell, it's easier to sleep!
Happy Birthday!

There are no suitable comments for the next poem.
It just describes how things are.

LIVING WITH CHEMOTHERAPY
AND A TRACHEOTOMY

Tied to the bed, tied to the drip.
Drink more water, sip after sip,
One more nebulizer, one more test!
Don't do that, Nurse knows best!

Don't let the boredom get you down!
Don't let your face fall to a frown!
Smile at the Doctors, laugh with the Nurse!
Remember the others who are a great deal worse.

Got through the first day! Hooray! Hooray!
Haven't been sick, what a good day!
Not coughing a lot, no sores in the mouth!
All's very well, North and South!

Having cancer is hard, particularly on close relatives. It saddened me to see the reactions of my wife and children.

MY WIFE MY CANCER

She worries too much!
Love driven anxiety!
Dominates her life,
Colours her perception.
And I worry that she,
will not cope with the bad days.
She is brave, she is courageous
But I am her Achilles' heel.
I have too much respect to lie
Or embellish the facts.
She will know the truth as it is.
And I will support her to accept.

*There is always pain. You can't get away from it. The
prescribed morphine dulls the edge but you can't just keep
taking it, so you accept what comes.*

PAIN

This pain has the purity of hard shining steel,

It has a truth, a power, as it tears my body apart.

There is a beauty in a pain so sharp there is no
  compromise.

So welcome it, sink into it and let it have its way.

And when it passes, breathless, gasp for air.

Recognize the clarity of the statement such pain makes,

And thank the fates you still are alive.

All the time I was in hospital I sang 'St. James Infirmary Blues' using words that I wrote myself. It helped during the difficult moments. By the way T2-c is a medical term indicating the stage the cancer has reached. If you're not a jazz blues fan, don't worry about it! Just read the damn thing and try to sense the rhythm. So here goes! Can you sense the beat?

THE POOLE INFIRMARY BLUES

(with apologies to St James Infirmary Blues)

Going on down to Poole Infirmary!
For to get my Chemo there.
Gonna take that drip; an armful!
To treat my big T2-C baby fair!

Now when my treatment's ended!
When the longed for time has come.
Gonna walk away from my baby.
Away from big T2-C baby fair.

Now I don't want no more babies!
Don't want no more big C fair.
Don't want no more chemo.
So cold, so sick, no hair!

My eldest daughter is one of the bravest and most principled persons I know. As a result she never ever gives up on anything.

NICKY

Steely determination; will to succeed.
Professional approach; emotional need.
Curly blond hair; figure a dream.
Needs recognition as part of the team.
Under the surface, lovely to know.
Wants to love you; doesn't dare show.
My little daughter, gone well beyond me.
My pride, my comfort, makes me carefree.
Don't look back Nicky my love.
Go forward now; take them by storm,
knowing I'm with you; your strong right arm.

I have granddaughter aged thirteen, living in America who attands a private school. The thirteen year old girls in eighth grade are difficult. Their mothers are worse, far worse. Woe be to anyone who does not agree with their interpretation of events. I wrote this poem as a 'tribute' to them.

THE WITCHES OF KING

If you go up to the school today,
Prepare for a big surprise
The eighth grade witches are coming to school
Are meeting there to gossip and spy
Today's the day they weave and lie.

But if you must peek
the sights you will see
Will shatter perception,
Your sense of fair play!

Laptops a' burning,
blackberries a' bubbling,
Coffee cups a' simmering,
gossip alight.
Starbucks been buzzing,
oh what an array.
The Mothers of Eighth Grade,
The Witches of King
are meeting today.

Oh beware, beware,
the Witches of King!
And all the trouble,
they only can bring.
With a little word here,
a whisper there.
No pity to spare.

Truth in the trash can,
Victim take care.
Speculate now,
exaggerate soon.
Make a good story,
twist that old tune,
Pick on the Victim.
Cry crocodile tears!
My daughter is innocent,
misled by her peers.
Both Mothers and Daughters
Are throwing their spears.

We really can't tell you,
shouldn't say that,
But it's so much fun,
being a cat.
Watch for the claws,
the nasty asides.
The innocent eyes,
while they utter their lies.
Pretending they're speaking
words to the wise

The Mothers agree
we should be less involved.
Let the girls sort it out,
Mothers absolved.
It's not us to blame,
what can we do?
We all have daughters
hard to control.
What we can't work out
Is what is our role?

Their stories are substitutes
For inadequate lives
Spent in luxury
sharpening their knives
To push in the back
as a nasty surprise,

To former friends
and enemies too
The Witches of King
will get on to you too.

ABOUT AUTUMN

*I am always most aware of the passing of the seasons
and I find the passage of Autumn to Winter depressing.
It is Autumn when we should contemplate all
that happened in the Spring and Summer
but we don't, we just get moody..*

AUTUMN

This autumn day is moleskin grey.
Silent, soft, rain, drifting down;
adding to already drenched land.
Trees hang heavy, leaves limply drip,
slow, heavy, shining, crystal drops.
Nature is showing her jewels.

In dark corners between the trees,
a mist has formed and unmoving,
waits to enfold the unwary.
Summer's tangled growth, dying now,
bends toward wet glistening grass.
Nature is holding her breath.

Later an ashen sun peeps through
and stirs a whispering wind to life.
The trees begin to move with gentle rhythm,
causing their dewy pearls to drop.
The first fingers of cold start to grip.
Autumn is leaving.

*There are particular nights in early Autumn when
the skies are clear and the air is still warm after
a sunny day. This, for me, is a magical time.*

NIGHT

Night whispering into dark night,
Warm and embracing, without light.
You can feel the friendly velvet quiet,
soft and smooth, gossamer cold.
Then the moon begins to show,
all that daylight left aglow.
The sunshine marriage is over.
All that remains are shadowed ends,
of nature's once beautiful things.

Give me softly, obscure, shadows,
where all is not proud, shining bright,
but merging gently into night.
Then I am at peace, safe,
closer to my imagined God.

A small poem about my feelings for
this particular time of year.

THOUGHTS OF AUTUMN

Clear Mountain Air.

Rain gently falling,

On glossy leaves.

Trees heavy and moist,

Whisper.

I am content.

THE CHRISTMAS POEMS

*Every Christmas day for the past twenty years
I have given my wife a new poem. They are always directed
at her and reflect our life together and
our love for each other. As such they are
very personal and emotional.
My wife has her own copies, which she treasures
and frequently reads. She has given her permission
for some of these poems to be reproduced
here. I hope you like them.*

This first poem; 'JAN' was the first of the Christmas Poems.
It tells the story of the most significant event of my life. It
was March 8th. 1952. I had played Rugby that afternoon
and I was tired and had a black eye! It was a last minute
decision to attend the school dance.
March 8th. has remained our most important
anniversary ever since.

JAN

Looking back; musing, reminiscing.
I remember when I met you.
You were so beautiful, so serene,
with lovely eyes and lovely smile.
But you had friends, superior friends:
with steady lives, sure of their way.
And I, clumsy, poor, unsure,
not knowing what to say.

Yet I won you, you were mine;
for the whole of the school dance.
I was so proud, so very proud,
I needed to stop the band!
Just to shout: She's with me! With me!
She doesn't mind my faults.
She doesn't mind that I can't dance,
can't speak with confidence.

I babbled nonsense all the night,
yet you listened and you listened.
With your enigmatic smile,
Such a beguiling mysterious smile;
A secret all your own.
Yet you agreed to see me!
To see ME! The very next weekend!

I had a girl to call my own; my very own.
To love, worship, cherish, to listen to my soul.
I didn't care, I didn't see, Head Boy's superior sneer.
So you got yourself a girlfriend then!
Thank God that you're not queer.
Now, I could fight those dragons, climb those mountains.
Compete with all my peers.
Face the world and all it does.
Chase away my daily fears.

And now, so much later, so many hurts ago!
You still are with me, still are mine.
You still are beautiful, still serene.
With your sweet mysterious smile;
Your secret garden smile.
Despite the wounds, the scars of life
which mean you can't forget.
We have stayed as one; a loving one
and we are stronger yet.
I have slain those dragons, climbed those mountains,
though falling many times.
I've been to the top and back again,
Felt the betrayal of friend by friend,
Have hurt and cried in the depths of deep despair.
And many times have given up,
Oh God! Are you still there?
But here I am, still fighting life,
Still strong, still sure, still giving of my best.
Still holding to principles we hold dear.
Never taking less.

But really it is you my love,
supporting all the way.
Pushing me, pulling me, making me go on.
When many times I would have quit,
wounded and afraid.

To blame my God, to curse my luck,
but never blame myself.
You are my strength, my blood, my mind.
My very life itself.
So now my wife, perhaps, perhaps,
you can see yourself, as I see you.
And understand the love I feel.
The peace; the strength I take from you.
Why I can still get up and try,
for more and better things!
'Cause I love you now, as I did then,
have always done and will in years to come.

*The following Christmas I continued the theme that
I owed everything to Jan. I make no apologies, I could not
help myself. I was in a place where I was consumed
by gratitude and guilt.*

I SEE YOU AS A GENTLE ROCK

I see you as a gentle rock,
Upon which the angry sea of my life breaks.
A firm and stable influence,
That overcomes my storms and gives me peace.

When I write my poetry, produce my art.
You are my muse, my inspiration.
I have no artistic life, except from you.
So every day I thank the God that made you mine.
It is true I use and abuse your loving soul.

The destructive side of me has still to know.
How far I can push your love for me.
I hate myself for testing you
And wonder why I do such things.

I know you care, else why would you stay?
My kinder side mostly dominates, thank God.
The side that only wants to honour and revere.
But the dark side must always have its time.

But you sweet wife understand all this and yet you care.
And still you soothe my torment; nurse my despair.
Bathe the wounded spirit and stand me up once more.
To try again to find an inner peace.

*The following year I wrote the poem which
is presented below. Reading it now together with
the two previous poems I realise how self obsessed
I was. The poetry betrays much about me when
really I wanted it to be all about Jan. However
I have resisted the temptation of a rewrite.*

LOOKING BACK

When first he met her, she overwhelmed him.
His passion, all-consuming, he drowned,
in her radiance and simple beauty.
Years later; he would wonder,
at that single event, which changed his life.
He would think back, savour the memory:
of when he realised she could be his.
After that; he never needed to remember,
the time before he met her and how it felt to be alone.

In the years that followed, she made him better
than he thought he was or ever deserved to be.
She taught him to trust, to love and not to doubt.
She drove away his angry, protective, cynicism.
It cost her much to stay supporting him,
but it was a price she gladly paid.
So many times he told her how he loved her,
But she never asked of him to show that love.
The love he had for her alone.

Now he looks back to where driving ambition
spawned those deceitful twins, success and failure.
Their life: full of incident and reckless adventure.
He, always seeking more of what he felt was right,
without ever considering the cost for her.

Never once asking, if she would pay the price.
But of course she always did, as he knew she would.
Leaving him wondering in sorrow at what he'd done.
Full of grateful humility.

Did he change, did he learn? No, he never did.
Even now he never stops to count the cost,
or doubt that she might not support the things he does.
But, once in a while, he stops to think,
And his intuition tells him what he has always assumed,
That perhaps, perhaps, she loves and supports him;
For what he is, not what he thinks he ought to be?
And he thanks the fates, for the time long past.
When the dice rolled for him.

Due to the pressures arising from our life in Lagos things had been difficult in the months leading up to Christmas.

LOVE LIVES

You can't put conditions on love.
Can't say you will:
or you won't.
To be in love, is not an act of conscious will,
it just happens.
And when it does,
it consumes you.

To stay in love, is something, you can decide.
You have a choice,
to stay in love, or not.
Love is such a delicate flower,
easily withered, by the creeping paralysis,
of easy familiarity and everyday dull
and ordinary things.

Love needs dedicated nurturing,
once the excitement dies,
and loving becomes a duty,
not joyous exploration.
Love needs the freshness of new excitements.
Selfless thoughts for each other.
Trying to please, in new ways.

We have kept our love alive.
It is stronger now than ever.
Sometimes it required emotional surgery.
There are bleeding memories,
buried deep in a cemetery of dreams.
Defeated ambitions put aside.
Never mentioned.

But we are like the finest sword,
tempered by fire,
strong, resilient.
Taking pleasure and support from each other.
Wrapped together in our private world,
we have become welded together,
never to break apart.

So, thank you my love,
for everything you've been,
and all that you've done,
and all that you have ever given me.
Over the years,
you have made me,
into someone better than I was,
able to appreciate,
your perfect love.

My mind works in images. This particular year I was struggling as usual to express how I felt about Jan. Suddenly it occurred to me that I could express my feelings in images.

IMAGINE

Imagine,
The purity of cold, crystal clear
drops of water,
falling from a frost filled tree;
the bright sun softly melting winter's grip.

Imagine,
The overwhelming consuming heat
flowing
from an angry volcano.
With a burning, all consuming, fire.

Imagine,
The overwhelming power
of a storm at sea
and you being helpless,
tossed wherever Nature wills.

Imagine,
The soft kiss of a sweet summer wind,
gently rustling the trees,
Shading flowers from a gentle sun,
Bright colours painted against the green.

Imagine,
Resting secure within your Mothers' arms.
The soft, pillowy warmth of her breast:
protecting you,
giving comforting safety.

Imagine,
The echoing peace of a giant cathedral;
You sitting, overawed.
In the presence of the great and good,
as troubles melt away and disappear.

Imagine,
The sinking excitement, before your marriage.
The thrill of holding your firstborn child.
The quiet satisfaction of winning through.

If you can imagine, all these things,
then you must know what you mean to me.
These are the feelings you give to me.
This was your dowry, your wedding gift.

The problem with writing a series of love poems to a much loved wife, is that the subject matter is limited. This particular year I was stuck, without inspiration. Then, at the last moment, it occurred to me that my wife had only her own memories, of our wedding day. I decided to tell her how it was from my point of view. After six and a half long years our wait was over. Our wedding was at St. Ethelreda's Church, Hatfield, Hertfordshire on September 13th. 1958. I should explain that many of Jan's Welsh relatives attended as you will see from the poem.

THE LONG WAIT IS OVER

We began, at The Eight Bells.
A quick drink,
to steady the nerve.
After; we climbed the hill,
past the houses full of history.
Almost at the top,
the church.
Centuries old,
a testament to Man's reverence.
A fitting place,
to promise myself,
to a special other.

That day
the sun was shining.
It seemed,
as if the world was smiling.
I walked into the church,
best man at my side,
and hat in hand,
took long slow strides.

I was trying to seem,
dignified and solemn,
when all I wanted to do was
dance and sing.

All about,
rustles and whispers, revealed,
hands shaken,
friendships renewed.
Hats and dresses noted,
dissected, costed and
entered in the gossip record.
Those memories would be taken out
and enjoyed in the valleys,
over tea and lava bread.

The wedding car climbed slowly,
driver in grey uniform,
passenger in white,
holding her father's hand,
looking straight ahead.
He sitting upright,
holding tight, tears held back.

She was slender, graceful,
in Chantilly lace,
veil in place,
bright eyed,
shining from within.

I sat in front,
best man at my side,
Six years of waiting,
about to end.

No more,
lonely, long walks home,
to face the ache of lonely nights.
Parents' objections
overcome.
Accepted
but not respected,
except by her.

The wedding march.
The bride was at the door,
with maids and train.
She was on her way,
to join me.
Stepping with the music,
slow and steady,
proud and erect.

I stood to the front
knees trembling,
careful to look ahead,
not to look back.

I sensed her stand beside me,
placing her hand on mine.
I could see her face,
her eyes,
moist and shining,
her smile,
small and tight.
The vicar stood before us.
'Dearly beloved,
we are gathered together
in the sight of God
to bless this union...........'

I never heard,
another word, until.
'Do you take this woman?'
'Oh yes, yes.'
I wanted to shout.
'For ever.'
I recall, slipping the ring,
upon her finger.
And then, it was over.

'I now pronounce you
man and wife.'
Her veil was folded back.
She was beautiful.
and I was dreaming,
and I never woke up.
And fifty years on,
I am still dreaming.

All I can say about the next poem is that
it is true in every aspect.

YOU TOOK CONTROL

When I was a young man I looked at the girls,
Some were beauties, some were pearls.
They promised much the blonds, the reds
They would twirl their skirts, offer their beds.
Sometimes I thought I would give them a try,
But I never did, I was just too shy.
Too afraid what others might think.
Happy to forget it, have another drink!
"They were never quite right, never quite so."
So one by one, they just had to go!

Then along came you, an ordinary girl,
Yet five minutes later, my heart's in a whirl,
Enslaved by your charm, you took control,
And all was quite right; all was just so.
I had to hang on, never let go.
I lost all control, I was weak with desire.
Unable to deal with the unquenchable fire.
Nerves stretched: life on a high wire.
Lucky for me you remained in my life,
And you became my beautiful wife.

*I was running my own business in Nigeria. I was
struggling with one setback after another. Within
the space of five weeks we endured two armed robberies
and were physically and mentally shaken up. We came
back to England for a week. My daughter suggested
that we should retire immediately. We did! It was a short,
sharp decision. We left everything behind. We never went
back to Lagos. No regrets, no recriminations, just relief.
The following Christmas I wrote the following poem.*

RETIREMENT

I stood up high upon the cliffs,
watching the cloudy, rainy, winds,
blowing seabirds o'er angry waves.
They seem to know of where they fly
but still are gusted here and there.
At last they reach their sheltered nest,
fussing down with pompous wriggles.
Proud, content, 'fore further struggle.

Our life together has been like that.
Buffeted by the winds of fate,
blowing us o'er the stormy sea.
Away from safe and sure haven.
Older now, wiser, wanting less.
No need to challenge wind and stress.
Risk random gust, capricious storm.
We too can settle down content.

It's the first time since we first met.
We can live, loving, together.
Each for the other, one for one.
No work, binding obligations,

to tear us apart. Say goodbye.
And if we are not quite so active,
quite so spry, not so attractive.
It doesn't matter, no, not at all.

A love like ours improves with age.
Growing mellow, ripe, richly deep,
yielding fragrant fruits, we can share.
Suck the juice of life, sweet affair.
No conscience, no guilt, we do deserve,
the overwhelming joy of life in love.
So let's enjoy our future life,
My gentle, sweet and patient wife.

There is a touch of plagiarism in this next poem since it was inspired by a Tina Turner song. However I hope that you will enjoy my interpretation which accurately describes my feelings.

I WOULD BREAK EVERY RULE

Every journey I take through life,
Brings me so much closer to you.
I'm starting to feel
I'm so much in love,
I would break every rule.

Every time when I look at you,
I don't care if I act like a fool.
I can see everything that;
I ever might want,
So I would break every rule.

So now that you know the score,
About how I'm feeling for you.
You'd better stay cool, don't step away!
Just be there for me every day.

I will be your slave,
Give you everything;
you might desire
Loving you so,
I'm trapped in your spell,
About to break every rule

Every moment is precious to me,
When we're together as one.
We will see off the world,
See our happiness build;

If you're very close to me,
So no one can come between.
And I can probably say,
And you can probably tell,

In the fullness of time;
Being together,
We will break every rule.

The next poem was written at a time when our future
was very uncertain. I was trying to recover from
a serious illness as well as major business set backs.
I was holding on, but for a long time, living had not been
a particularly attractive proposition. The result was that
when I sat down to write the Christmas Poem I had
only dark thoughts. Then, my wife, after
I had sat at the meal table silent for some time asked
me what was I thinking. I replied that I was thinking
about her and then said casually and thoughtlessly,
'I am always thinking about you'. The following
poem was born at that instant.

YOU ARE ALWAYS IN MY MIND!

You are always in my mind
Feeding my understanding.
Every decision that I take;
Everything that I do,
Is influenced by thoughts of you.

For fifty years you have cast your spell
And I have been entranced.
Your song entwines around me
The magical music that you sing
Is the music that I've danced.

For all that time I've been enthralled.
Rapt in the spell you weaved.
But, what God gives, so God takes back.
'And so we pay for our good luck
'Til we finish, balance even.

Or do we?

You have been my lover,
My comfort and my solace.
And tho' any pain is hard to bear
When loving hand and heart's not there.
I have found it easier, knowing that you care.

We all need someone to come to,
When we fight to stay alive.
We all are lonely inside our heads,
Inside mine can be so scary,
When we cannot be together.

We talk, we touch, we feel, we share,
grow closer, as respect brings love;
need brings desire.
When mixed together,
they are overwhelming.
It makes a sometimes raw emotion,

So deep it hurts and cannot be assuaged.
That spell you wove entrapping me,
Still is working strong.
A living, growing, changing, thing,
Coping with all that's hard to bear.
More valuable, every happy year.

You say I am the shining star
Wrong, quite wrong, your aura outshines mine.
You are my summer; autumn; winter; spring!
You my darling are just.........
my everything!

THE YOUNGER GENERATION

One of the great delights of my life occurred when I discovered that my middle daughter was writing poetry. I cannot resist including one of her best efforts, with her permission of course.

ON REACHING FORTY

Everyone told me:
"When you reach forty
it will be the time to take stock ".
A time to accept the watershed;
the transition;
to a quieter, wiser, time.
A time where youth has departed
never to return except in others
A time to be at peace with my life.

Well, I never found that peace
I was unaware of the transition
And I felt just as young,
My life remained the same.
I enjoy my life just as much as I ever did.

Times gone by are memories, nothing more.
There is nothing, I would go back to
Except perhaps a different start:
no, not even that:
were it to mean I wouldn't have,
the many good things I have now.

If asked, I would say that reaching forty
is a time for celebration.
when you finally get the respect
you have deserved for many years.
A time when remarks about being past it,
over the hill, are just self-protecting signs of envy.

It's the start of the more interesting,
fun part of life,
with nothing much more to learn or study.
Time to use the experience gained,
in those frantic early years
Time to please yourself.

*This next poem was written by Max, my Grandson,
aged 10. The remarkable thing is that he wrote
it without help. I was there and saw him do it.*

CLEANING THE HOUSE

Brushes and brooms, My Oh MY.
My Mum's making me do this, why oh why?
Grabbing the supplies with lots of muscle.
Why does this involve so much hassle?
All I have to do now is find the spray.
To be honest I would prefer to pay.
Thinking of paying my friend.
Good thing his back is able to bend.
It's time for me to start to clean.
I bet you my Mum, feels like a queen.
I see a big puddle just like a bay.
Oh, if only I could move away.
Wait, did I see the print of a paw on the floor.
Seriously Mum I can't do any more.
I can officially say I hate cleaning the house.
I would rather go to school wearing a blouse.

Not to be outdone by his little brother, William aged 15 sent me a poem. This was a quite unexpected pleasure. It was inspired by a discussion at school on paradoxes. It is deep and it needs three or four readings for full understanding. As I told him, 'this poem is not for lazy minds'.

MUCH WISDOM IS IGNORANCE

Much wisdom is ignorance
To the many undeserving.
He has the intelligence,
Bounding through life, observing.

Through tireless trial and error,
Always evolving, for good.
Yet through daylight, comes a terror.
Resistance prompts war, it prompts blood.

Blood spills and battles are lost.
Ignorance breeds from wise blood.
A trap! encased in frost,
A wise man, left in mud.

Wisdom creates the fissure,
Filled with deep, green ignorance.
Forced into hate and anger.
Much wisdom often breeds a dunce.

Much wisdom is ignorance
Though wisdom breeds arrogance.
Is knowledge your preference?
Or will you find a balance?

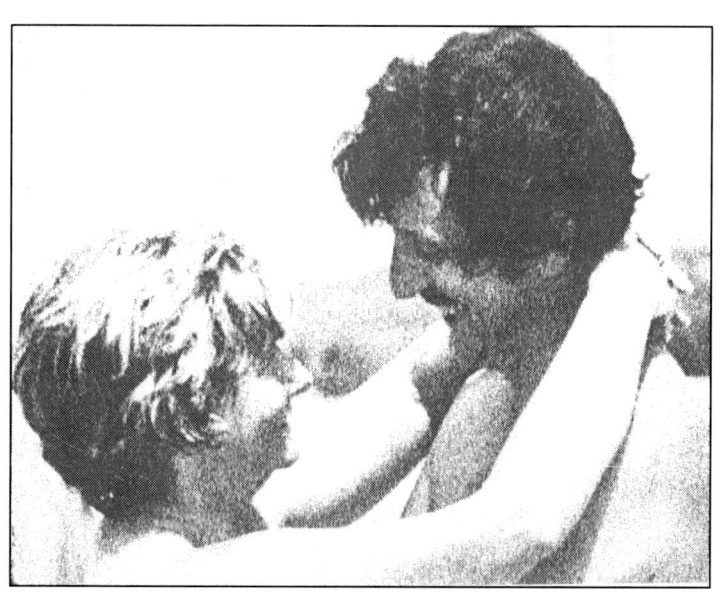

Lightning Source UK Ltd.
Milton Keynes UK

176596UK00002B/15/P